Sarah,
This little book spoke to me in your voice. Love....
Fredi

the LITERARY GARDENER

WALTER CHANDOHA

WILLOW CREEK PRESS

Published in 1997
by Willow Creek Press
P.O. Box 147
Minocqua, WI 54548

For information on other Willow Creek Press titles, call
1-800-850-WILD

**Library of Congress
Cataloging-in-Publication Data**
Chandoha, Walter
    The literary gardener / Walter Chandoha.
    p.   cm.
    ISBN 1-57223-083-5
    1. Gardening. 2. Gardening--Literary collection. I.
Title.
SB455.C465   1997
820.8'0364--dc21   97-28061
                                     CIP

Design by Heather M. McElwain

Printed in the United States of America

FOREWORD

arly in my career as a freelance photographer, I began gardening for edibles, to feed my wife and growing family. As my family continued to grow, so did my gardens and my knowledge of gardening. We ate fruits and vegetables fresh from the garden throughout the growing season; and with dry storage, freezing and canning, our gardens fed us into the winter as well. What garden skills I've acquired in the past thirty or so years have come primarily from books, whose authors, both classic and contemporary, share with the world their knowledge and wisdom, philosophy and humor, frustrations and achievements.

Over the years, as I became more and more involved in gardening I gradually acquired a horticultural library. Wherever I traveled I'd seek out new and second-hand book stores looking for current and out-of-print volumes on some facet of gardening, not necessarily the how-to's (after all, how many books do we need on how to grow lettuce?) but the why's and the philosophy of gardening, the history of plants, their origins, how they were named, myths and folklore surrounding them, their medicinal qualities, monographs on a single species.

As I continued reading and learning, my interest in garden photography, like my gardening, broadened from pictures of just vegetables to the whole gamut of just about everything that grows or is part of gardens and landscapes. Then one day it occurred to me that I could combine my garden photography with words of classic and contemporary writers, as I did years ago in *The Literary Cat.*

Not only are some of my favorite classic garden writers included in *The Literary Gardener:* Vita Sackville-West, Gertrude Jekyll, Charles Dudley Warner and Russell Page but also authors whose fame is in areas other than in gardening but who have been involved in gardening: Colette, Thomas Jefferson, Jerzy

Kosinski, Arthur Miller and Gertrude Stein. And I was especially pleased to have found a good bit of humor among such writers as Ogden Nash (who it appears to have written on a whole gamut of subjects), Reginald Arkell, Hilaire Belloc, Karel Capek, Peter deVries, S.J. Perelman and my good friend Dereck Williamson.

Selecting text and photographs to go into a book like *The Literary Gardener* might be compared to deciding what to plant in the vegetable garden each year. From a garden catalog — or multiple catalogs — selections must be made. There are so many choices, and because space in the garden is limited, many excellent vegetables are not even considered. What we do grow in our gardens is very personal and subjective.

It's the same way with a book like *The Literary Gardener*. It's personal and subjective. And like a garden, with its limited amount of space, a book has a limited number of pages. Choices had to be made. Many excellent writings had to be eliminated because of space considerations. Ultimately, what I selected is what I liked. I concurred with the philosophy and thinking of some of the writers, others told me something new; maybe a piece shed new light on an old subject or something obvious was retold in an entertaining way; or I selected others because I was inspired, entertained, amused, humbled or enlightened.

— *Walter Chandoha*

ALL WILL BE WELL

n a garden . . . growth has its season. There are spring and summer, but there are also fall and winter. And then spring and summer again. As long as the roots are not severed, all is well and all will be well.

— Jerzy Kosinski, *Being There*

SEASONS OF CONSTANT CHANGE

There is a midsummer. There is a midwinter. But there is no midspring or mid-autumn. These are the seasons of constant change. Like dawn and dusk they are periods of transition. But like night and day and day and night they merge slowly, gradually. As Richard Jefferies once wrote, broken bits of summer can be found scattered far into the shortening days of fall. Only on calendars and in almanacs are the lines of division sharply defined.

— Edwin Way Teale, *Autumn Across America*

Anyone Can Be A Gardener

nyone can be a gardener. It's simply a matter of choice. On the day you find your-self fretting about the first frost or ruminating about rhododendron color, the day you say to yourself, "I'm a gardener" — you are one. You need no degrees or doc-torates, no accumulations of blue ribbons at a prestigious Iris Competition, no title bestowed by an intimidating gardening society, no personnel official to declare "you're in," nor any special knowledge of pH factors or compost heaps. What is essential is training your vision to see beyond what's already there; having enough strength to haul around a gar-den cart filled with fifty pound bags; and money, because you can't start planting without any plants . . .

— Dianne Benson, *Dirt*

SPRING

Now 'tis spring, and weeds are shallow-rooted;
Suffer them now and they'll o'ergrow the garden.

— William Shakespeare, *Henry IV*

DICTAMNUS OR DIANTHUS

t is always trouble to get plants. In March the nurseryman usually doesn't send you your order, because it may freeze, and the seedlings are not yet up; in April he does not send them either, because he has too much on hand, and in May because he has generally sold out.

"There are no primulas left, but I will send you mullein instead; it has got yellow flowers as well." But sometimes it happens that the post brings a package of seedlings which you ordered. Hurrah! Right here in this bed I want something very high among monk's-hood and larkspurs; we will certainly put dictamnus there, the plant which is also called dittany or the burning bush; the seedlings which they have sent are rather tiny, but they will grow like wildfire. A month passes and the seedlings don't grow very much; they look like very short grass — if they were not dictamnus you would say they are dianthus. We must water them properly to make them grow; and look here, they have something like pink flowers.

"Look," says the owner of the garden to an expert visitor; "isn't that a small dictamnus?"

"You mean dianthus," says the guest.

"Of course, dianthus," says the host eagerly; "it was a slip. I was just thinking that among these high perennials a dictamnus would look better, don't you think so?"

— Karel Capek, *The Gardener's Year*

JOHNNY APPLESEED

 f Johnny Appleseed were to visit present-day suburbia, he would weep. In most yards he would be likely to find not a fruit-laden apple tree, but a flowering crab-apple, cherry, plum or peach tree — none bearing fruit. Fifty years ago, he would have had more luck. Our grandmothers usually kept a fruiting apple, cherry or peach tree in their front yard, and grew vegetables and herbs near the kitchen door. The trees not only were beautiful at blossom time, but they provided fruits to be eaten fresh and preserved for the months ahead. Some vegetables, too, provided pleasure to the eye as well as provender for the pantry. But Grandma's main interest was food. Beauty in a producing plant was a bonus, not a requirement.

— Rosalind Creasy, *The Complete Book of Edible Landscaping*

our seeds in the hole,
One for the rook,
One for the crow,
One for to rot,
And one for to grow.

— Leon Uris, *Trinity*

MIST OF MORNING

How many a plant or flower is not doggedly uprooted, mowed or sprayed to death simply because it bears the name of weed, while another no better is patiently cultivated because the way has been semantically paved in its favor. Take the lowly chickweed which we hound from our lawns like a common criminal. Suppose its white-flowered variants were called something like "mist of morning," its blue, say "Mary's eyes," while the pachysandra now preferred as a ground cover bore the name of packweed. How the latter would be plucked with sweat and curses, while we trod carefully over the grass lest we trample the newly sprung Mary's eyes or mist of morning.

— Peter deVries, *Reuben, Reuben*

HOW MY GARDEN AND I GROW

The best gardeners are those who most graciously accept the task of waiting and watching. Because I was so new to this idea, I was the more profoundly moved when an answer came to me last spring. After a terrible disappointment in love, I had neglected my garden, watching it die a slow death until it reflected the bleakness I felt. Then one day, believing I would never find pleasure in anything again, I absently lifted up the trunk of my dead banana tree. Six new little trees were springing up out of the ground from the roots. It had never been dead. It was only dormant. Might I be dormant too. A year has passed and my garden has been tilled and cultivated and mined with dozens of bulbs, all generously dusted with bonemeal. I have planned an explosion of color and pattern for spring. We must weather our winters, whether of ice or discontent. We must hold on and wait for the thaw.

— Lisa Germany, *Self* magazine

MAPLE SEEDS

This spring we gathered up several bushels — millions — of seeds from under our maple trees, every one of which might have made a new tree fifty feet tall, to live for a century or more, and itself produce countless billions of seeds. Yet not one of the seeds we gathered will ever grow; they decay on my compost heap. It is a wearying thought — the vast fecundity of nature, wherein birth is an infinitesimal chance; wherein growth after birth is only a remote possibility; wherein final maturity is not short of a miracle.

— David Grayson, *The Countryman's Year*

GARDEN GHOSTS

hosts walk in most gardens. Usually they are called up by sentiment. Every spring I carry a cluster of pansies and lilies of the valley to the secretary of a friend of mine because, on her way to work, she often pauses by the fence to remark that her mother grew and loved pansies and lilies of the valley. A local businessman frequently stops to make the same remark about the morning glories that festoon the trellis over our front door.

— Buckner Hollingsworth, *Gardening on Main Street*

hey are . . . blessed with the ability to see green where there is but rock and cinder, height where it's flat, fullness from bare roots, and hope in a seed packet. They are proud scalers of steep learning curves. Their mastery of design is mostly instinctual. They know their garden intimately, like a lover or a child, know its need for light and dark, its vulnerability to wind or damp. They watch life-and-death dramas play out in their ground every day. They describe their passion in lovesick terms: hooked, obsessed, addicted, crazy, mad. They swallow disappointments and carry on; laugh at the naivete of their mistakes. They've learned that getting the soil right often counts more than getting the plants right. Impatient, they're always trading time for money, size for number.

— Dorothy Kalins, *Garden Design* magazine

THE LILIES OF THE FIELD

onsider the lilies of the field, how they grow; they toil not, neither do they spin: And yet I say unto you, That even Solomon in all his glory was not arrayed like one of these.

— Matthew, *New Testament*

Like children who seem to grow up overnight, our gardens surprise us in the spring. There may still be a chill in the air and random spots of snow on the ground, but the apple blossoms are more than ready to go to work, and the daffodils and tulips are waving their arms like kids who have the answer. Since it's probably too soon — and too muddy — to start the heavy-duty work outside, enjoy the show. Let nature tell us what it knows.

— *Martha Stewart Living* magazine

A GARDENER LEARNS

know nothing whatever of many aspects of gardening and very little of a great many more. But I never saw a garden from which I did not learn something and seldom met a gardener who did not, in one way or another, help me.

— Russell Page, *The Education of a Gardener*

PLANNING THE GARDEN

ome the middle of April, the family invariably gets the urge to see the old man beating his brains out in the garden patch. It's funny, but nobody ever gets the urge to see him snoozing on the lounge. If he isn't staggering under a wheelbarrow of manure or grubbing in the subsoil, he's a leper.

Planning a garden takes place, as all the handbooks advise, long before the frost is out of the ground, preferably on a night recalling Keat's "Eve of St. Agnes," with hail lashing the windows. The dependents reverently produce the latest seed catalogue and succumb to mass hypnosis. "Look at those radishes — two feet long!" every one marvels . . . A list of staples is speedily drawn up: Brussels sprouts the size of a rugby, eggplant like captive balloons, and yams. Granny loves corn fritters; a half acre is allotted to Golden Bantam. The children need a pumpkin for Halloween, and let's have plenty of beets, we can make our own lump sugar. Then someone discovers the hybrids — the onion crossed with a pepper or a new vanilla-flavored turnip that plays the "St. James Infirmary Blues." When the envelope is finally sealed, the savings account is a whited sepulcher and all we need is a forty-mule team to haul the order from the depot.

— S.J. Perelman, *Acres and Pains*

GOOD WEEDS

The lore of weeds is in many ways as interesting as the history of grains, for many plants now considered objectionable were once of great value. In our own time we are seeing honeysuckle, which was one of America's most prized vines, becoming a vicious weed that crowds out all other vegetation that it invades. The troublesome American daisy was first known as "day's eye." The word was later combined into *dayseye*, and finally to *daisy*. A farm weed now, it was in earlier times prized as first-quality hay material. Dandelion is a bad word in any lawn-maker's vocabulary, yet originally it was an introduced and prized plant: its leaves and buds were used for boiled greens or for "wilted salad," and its roots when ground were used as a good coffee substitute. Summer was "officially in" with dandelion-picking time; but few people in our time have ever tasted dandelions. A beverage may be made from dandelions that was once called Lion-tooth Wine, a name which recalls the plant's original name, *dent de lion*, after the lion-toothed shape of its leaf. Dandelion wine is still considered a fine tonic for elderly people.

— Eric Sloane, *The Seasons of America Past*

GRASS IS ELEGANT

rass is always the most elegant, more elegant than rocks and trees, trees are elegant and so are rocks but grass is more so.

Gertrude Stein, *The World is Round*

FLOWER FRAGRANCE

know next to nothing about fragrance. A year of trying to learn about it has left me as ignorant as ever, beyond a few simple facts that everybody knows, such as that a moist, warm day with a touch of sun will bring out fragrance, that hot sun and drought can destroy it, that frost sometimes releases it, and that rain will draw out the good chlorophyll scents of grass and foliage. The commonest complaint one hears today from amateur gardeners is that modern flowers, particularly roses, are losing their fragrance, thanks to the hybridizers' emphasis on form and color, and it had seemed to me, too, that many flowers smell less sweet than they used to. Sweet peas . . . I remember them as sweeter still in my aunts' flower garden of long ago . . . Iris . . . a gardening friend with a particularly alert nose remembers the old-fashioned "flag lilies" of his childhood as very fragrant. Lilacs: The common single farmyard lilac for me has the headiest spring scent of all . . .

Katherine S. White, *Onward and Upward in the Garden*

SNOWDROPS

 ome gardeners think of the winter Aconite as the first flower of spring but I have never done much with those pleasant little yellow flowers and the shooting of the Snowdrop leaves is my particular signal that spring, even if far away, will come in time. It is strange that no country name compares Snowdrops with bells for they are bell-like as they swing to and fro. How they do swing on those delicate threads which connect flower to stem. You'd think they would be torn off. But they can stand any gale that blows. They yield to the wind rather than oppose it. A tree may be blown down in the night but never a single Snowdrop head is blown off. Their strength is that they know when to give in. There is moral in that somewhere.

H.L.V. Fletcher, *Popular Flowering Plants*

I wandered lonely as a cloud
   That floats on high o'er vales and hills,
   When all at once I saw a crowd,
A host, of golden daffodils;
Beside the lake, beneath the trees
Fluttering and dancing in the breeze.

Continuous as the stars that shine
And twinkle in the milky way,
They stretched in never-ending line
Along the margin of a bay:
Ten thousand saw I at a glance,
Tossing their heads in sprightly dance.

— William Wordsworth, *I Wandered Lonely As A Cloud*

The Love of Dirt

o own a bit of ground, to scratch it with a hoe, to plant seeds, and watch their renewal of life — this is the commonest delight of the race, the most satisfactory thing a man can do.

— Charles Dudley Warner, *My Summer in a Garden*

CELESTIAL ORDER

Spring is one thing that man has never had a hand in, no hand at all. It is as remote from man as sunrise or the phases of the moon. This may be difficult to believe when you have a gardenful of daffodils and hyacinths and tulips planted by your own hand. But none of us can fend off an April frost, and none of us can make a tulip bulb grow and come to blossom by holding it in our hands. We have to commit it to the earth and trust to forces beyond human power or control.

Spring came before man was here to see it, and it will keep on coming even if man isn't here to see it sometime in the future. It is a matter of solar mechanics and celestial order. And for all our knowledge of astronomy and terrestrial mechanics, we haven't yet been able to do more than bounce a radar beam off the moon. We couldn't alter the arrival of Spring by one second if we tried.

— Hal Borland, *This Hill, This Valley*

SUMMER

To be an amateur vegetable gardener is to be spurred on by both artichokes that never appear and by summer squash that won't go away.

— Roger B. Swain, *Harrowsmith* magazine

THE EVER-OPEN DOOR

GOOD gardeners all will deprecate
The man who shuts his garden gate.

My garden gate is open wide,
And *any one* can walk inside

Except, of course, the ass who says:
"*My* lupins have been out for *days.*"

— Reginald Arkell, *Green Fingers*

A Sundial

I am a sundial, and I make a botch
Of what is done far better by a watch.

— Hilaire Belloc, *A Joy of Gardening*

THE MIXED-UP GARDEN

here is no reason why herbs and vegetables should not fit very well into an already existing garden pattern, either added to flower beds or in separate beds. The shapes, textures, and foliage colors of many kitchen garden plants add variety to flower-garden and lawn areas, and herbs in particular add fragrance to a pleasure garden. Lettuce, cabbage, or kale, for example, add rounded shapes and varied color in a low border. The green lacy foliage of carrots adds interest to the massed color of annuals such as petunias. Spiky leaves and delicate flowers of chives outline any garden area attractively and provide interesting as well as useful borders.

— Mary Mason Campbell, *Betty Crocker's Kitchen Garden*

MY GARDEN

he tomato, fastened to stakes, will shine with a thousand globes, enpurpled as June advances; see how many love-apples, violet aubergines and yellow pimentos, grouped in an old-fashioned convex border, will enrich my kitchen garden . . . There, garden, there! Don't forget you're going to feed me . . . I want you decorative, but full of culinary graces. I want you flower-filled, but not with those delicate flowers bleached by a single cricket-chirping summer's day. I want you to be green, but not with a relentless greenery of palms and cacti, the desolation of Monaco, that simulated Africa. Let the arbutus grow beside the orange and the bouganvillaea's violet torches clothe my walls. And let mint and tarragon and sage grow at their feet, tall enough for the dangling hand to bruise their branches and release their urgent perfume. Tarragon, sage, mint, savory, burnet — opening your pink flowers at noon, to close three hours later — truly I love you for yourselves — but I shan't fail to call on you for salads to go with boiled leg of mutton, to season sauces; I shall exploit you.

— Colette, *Places*

VEGETABLES OF THE RICH

A friend of mine once asked me: "Do you know the difference between the rich and well, you and me? Vegetables." "Vegetables?" "Vegetables!" At Babe Paley's table or Bunny Mellon's or Betsy Whitney's or Ceezie's — haven't you ever noticed how extraordinary the vegetables are? The smallest, most succulent peas, lettuce, the most delicate baby corn, asparagus, limas the size of cuticles, the tiny sweet radishes, everything so fresh, almost unborn — that's what you can do when you have an acre or so of greenhouses."

My friend's observation was true — a certain kind of hostess always does serve exceptional vegetables, though owning hot-houses is apparently not the answer, for most of this elegant produce is grown in ordinary, if extensively cared for, gardens. When I asked Mrs. Guest about this, she said: "The only thing I use hot-houses for is flowers and plants. Everything else is out of doors: raspberries, tomatoes, all that."

— Truman Capote, Introduction to C.Z. Guest's *First Garden*

A GRAY GARDEN

ne of the most exciting things about planning a garden is the many and varied ways there are to play with color — from the blending of great masses of color to highlighting the gemlike glow of a single blossom.

Even more subtle is the palette provided by the tones of the foliage. Plants have leaves not only in every imaginable shade of green, but in shades of red, purple, blue, gray — even white.

When you see its full design possibilities, foliage becomes much more than something that sprouts out of the stalk below the flowers, and the color scheme of your garden is not limited to a sea of green with bright spots of color in it. You can have a garden with almost no green at all — or with no flowers.

— Barbara Damrosch, *Theme Gardens*

WATER

ater makes a jungle; lack of it, a desert. Plenty of it makes one man a "born gardener" while another who shorts his garden on water wonders why he can't grow cucumbers and tomatoes the way they look in seed catalogs. The real secret of luxuriant gardens is plenty of water.

— Richard C. Davids, *Garden Wizardry*

WORKING WITH NATURE

The Natural Garden is a garden planted with species that are natural to their environments, species that would grow wild. Plants are chosen with an entire year, or years, in mind — they are not expected to work for just one season — and the garden design makes use of long-lasting natural materials. Thus the garden is beautiful year-round as well as being easy to maintain. Lawn is reduced to the minimum needed for recreation, shrubs bloom throughout and are seldom pruned, color comes from dependable perennials and easy-care hybrids, and spaces for entertaining are paved with permanent materials that match the resources in the landscape and require little care. Your garden is the product of a close collaboration between you and nature, in which what you want from the garden is met by the character of your particular location. Instead of fighting the elements to create the perfect lawn and formal garden, you work in partnership with nature to discover and enhance the best features of the land . . .

— Ken Druse, *The Natural Garden*

FOXGLOVE

Some of the common names of the foxglove, *Digitalis purpurea*, date back to early days when fairies and evil spirits were familiar presences, others have a Christian character. They are: folk's glove, witches' gloves, fairy gloves, fairy caps, fairy thimble, dead men's bells, bloody fingers and gloves of our lady. Because the plants are biennial, in their first year they produce only the basal rosette of leaves. During the second summer stems four feet high appear, bearing a spire two feet long of nodding two-lipped flowers that grow on one side of the stem. The entire plant is softly hairy. When grown in semishade or in sparse woods, conditions similar to its wild haunts, foxglove will self-sow freely . . .

— Helen M. Fox, *The Years in My Herb Garden*

LANDSCAPING IS DECORATING

andscaping is similar to decorating in some ways and dissimilar in others. For although the principles of balance and taste are fundamentally the same in both, inanimate objects stand still for us to mold. Whenever we deal with living things, however, we are confronted with unique and sometimes perverse reactions which have a way of subverting our plans. Moving and accommodating a plant to a new area presupposes an acquaintance with the plant's characteristic habits and needs thus providing a basis for correct planning and care.

— Frances Howard, *Landscaping with Vines*

BE BRUTAL AND IMAGINATIVE

ardening is largely a question of mixing one sort of plant with another sort of plant, and of seeing how they marry happily together; and if you see that they don't marry happily, then you must hoick one of them out and be quite ruthless about it.

That is the only way to garden; and that is why I advise every gardener to go round his garden now — (summer) and make note of what he thinks he ought to remove and what he wants to plant later on.

The true gardener must be brutal, and imaginative for the future.

— Vita Sackville-West, *A Joy of Gardening*

GARDENING AS OUTDOOR THEATER

Some gardeners, I believe, use gardening as outdoor theater, with themselves as directors. Some prefer the security of repeating a similar production year after year; they thrive on praise heaped on their efforts. Others prefer the challenge of new tableaux each year; the thrill of learning about new plants and how to fit them into the gardening environment is what gives them satisfaction. Some, in order to understand the plants who are players imbue them with human characteristics. They talk to them, praise them, interact with them, move them around the stage, change the lighting . . . but, ultimately, if they fail to perform, they reach for the stage hook.

— Jim Wilson, *Masters of the Victory Garden*

THE STEALTHY VINE

The problem of an outside plant going inside is common to quaint old stone houses held together with ivy. One day you will discover a little vine sneaking along the top of the bookshelf, unusual because there is no house plant on the bookshelf.

Take a deep breath. Examine the vine. Follow it along the wall. See where it comes through the crack between the stones. Go outside. See where it goes in through the crack between the stones.

Do not cut the vine off. If you do, two more vines will enter the house. Then four; then eight. Don't get a vine mad. Cooperate with it by stringing wire around the room. The vine will follow it, and it will get longer and longer.

Sometime late at night you will be able to hear it, growing.

— Dereck Williamson, *The Complete Book of Pitfalls*

MY MOTHER'S GARDEN

here was a tidy garden patch at the back of the house where mother grew chives, shallots, onions, radishes, some herbs and always a few hills of potatoes. She would insist on having these potatoes dug very early. She felt if you were going to eat new potatoes, you ate them small, cooked them little and gave them plenty of butter. Therefore, we ate potatoes the size of small marbles. Recently at a farmers' market in Lausanne, I found enough of these tiny potatoes to feast on with sentimental delight. Some restaurants ruin them by overcooking them in fat until they are hard and leathery. To be at their best, they should be cooked in their skins, which intensifies the flavor. Sometimes we ate them with their jackets and sometimes without. Occasionally Mother combined them with the tenderest of new peas from the garden, cooked for just a few minutes in a little water with lettuce leaves and butter. What a combination of flavors!

— James Beard, *Delights and Prejudices*

AUTUMN

O Autumn, laden with fruit, and stained
With the blood of the grape, pass not, but sit
Beneath my shady roof; there thou may'st rest
And tune thy jolly voice to my fresh pipe,
And all the daughters of the year shall dance!
Sing now the lusty song of fruits and flowers.

—— William Blake, *To Autumn*

MATURE GARDENS

Unlike people, gardens never strive for perpetual youth — they want to look old from the day they were born. Their greatest glory comes with maturity. New gardens try to look old before their time. They are in luck when old trees exist to help them out — even one tree out of scale and stature will give a garden a semblence of middle age before its first birthday.

— Thomas D. Church, *Gardens are for People*

THE JERUSALEM ARTICHOKE

his excellent plant food is native to the central part of our country but was culti-
vated in the East both by Indians and, later, by whites. It long ago escaped from
cultivation in this area and has become thoroughly naturalized, being fairly common in old fields, waste places and along roadsides. I seldom travel in September or early
October without seeing many clumps of Jerusalem artichokes growing along the roads or
on the railroad right of ways. The plant is mostly easily located when in flower, and that is
the time to select your foraging ground for later in the fall . . .

— Euell Gibbons, *Stalking the Wild Asparagus*

A Sense of Beauty

Sense of beauty is the gift of God, for which those who have received it in good measure can never be thankful enough. The nurturing of this gift through long years of study, observation, and close application in any one of the ways in which fine art finds expression, is the training of the artist's brain and heart and hand. The better a human mind is trained to the perception of beauty the more opportunities will it find of exercising this precious gift, and the more directly will it be brought to bear upon even the very simplest matters of everyday life, and always to their bettering.

— Gertrude Jekyll, *Colour Schemes for the Flower Garden*

THE ATTRACTIONS OF GARDENING

The attractions of gardening, I think, at least for a certain number of gardeners, are neurotic and moral. Whenever life seems pointless and difficult to grasp, you can always get out in the garden and *get something done*. Also, your paternal or maternal instincts come into play because helpless living things are depending on you, require training and discipline and encouragement and protection from enemies and bad influences. In some cases, as with squash and some cucumbers, your offspring — as it were — begin to turn upon you in massive numbers, proliferating more and more each morning and threatening to follow you into the house to strangle you in their vines. Zucchini tend to hide their fruits under broad leaves until they have become monster green phallic clubs to mock all men and subvert the women.

— Arthur Miller, *After the Spring House & Garden* magazine

NATURE IS SELECTIVE

Nature works no faster than need be. If she has to produce a bed of cress or radishes, she seems to us swift; but if it is a pine or oak wood, she may seem to us slow or wholly idle, so leisurely and secure is she . . . She knows that seeds have many other uses than to reproduce their kind. If every acorn of this year's crop is destroyed, or the pines bear no seed, never fear. She has more years to come. It is not necessary that a pine or an oak should bear fruit every year, as it is that a pea vine should.

— Henry David Thoreau, *Faith in a Seed*

Who, for lack of a garden, hasn't gathered armfuls of goldenrod to bring cheer into a bleak summer cottage or camp? Who, even *with* a garden, hasn't put a jar of goldenrod or asters on the porch in August? Thus, we think of it as common, yet goldenrod, whose Latin name is *Solidago*, is not a humble flower. It must have been taken to England from North America by the early British plant explorers, for American goldenrod had long held a cherished place in many an English herbaceous border. Now, ironically, it is being exported back to us and offered in the nursery catalogs as something very special.

— Katherine S. White, *Onward and Upward in the Garden*

WINDOWBOX GARDENING

any people get outdoor gardening fever when the days begin to lengthen but, unfortunately, have no garden. If, however, you have a window space that you don't have to give up to that mumbling monster, the air conditioner, it is perfectly possible to make a small outdoor plot with a window box. This can be a show piece of flowers or merely a place to grow a few tomatoes. Either way, it serves an invaluable purpose by enabling the gardenless gardener to stay in contact with the soil and the natural cycle of outdoor growth. In these times of pressure and tension, this can be more important to our inner well-being than perhaps we realize.

— Thalassa Cruso, *Making Things Grow*

HE DIGS, HE DUG, HE HAS DUG

ay not Eve needed Adam's pardon
For their eviction from the garden;
I only hope some power divine
Gets round to ousting me from mine.
On bended knee, perspiring clammily,
I scrape the soil to feed my family,
Untaught, unteachable, undramatic,
A figure sorry and sciatic.
I brood as patiently as Buddha,
Nothing comes up the way it shudda.
They're making playshoes of my celery,
It's rubbery, and purple-yellery,
My beets have botts, my kale has hives,
There's something crawly in my chives,
And jeering insects think it's cute
To swallow my spray and spit out my fruit.
My garden will never make me famous,
I'm a horticultural ignoramus,
I can't tell a stringbean from a soybean,
Or even a girl bean from a boy bean.

— Odgen Nash, *Versus*

WITH MY OWN HANDS

hen I go into the garden with a spade, and dig a bed, I feel such exhilaration and health that I discover that I have been defrauding myself all this time in letting others do for me what I should have done with my own hands.

— Ralph Waldo Emerson, *Greenprints*

THE FUTURE

he future, once we reach middle age, always seems daunting and it'll never take the course you expect it to anyway. Live for the here and now, then, if here and now seems good.

Let all your planning ahead be for your plants; a year ahead for annuals, two years ahead for biennials, an indefinite number of years ahead for the trees. Never take the 'I shan't see it' attitude. By exercising a little vision you will come to realize that the tree, which has a possible future, perhaps a great one, may be more important than yourself nearing your end. So it's worth thinking more about the tree and giving it a good start in life in the right position than about yourself, except in so far as is a great delight to see the tree responding and developing under your sympathetic treatment.

— Christopher Lloyd, *The Adventurous Gardener*

WINTER

. . . think a moment about a garden forever warm, forever growing, always green, with brilliant dots of color every day of the year — a garden that never rests. There would be no time to plan, no moments to quietly sit and reflect on the triumphs and failures of the preceding seasons, no chance for change.

And the muted colors of winter would be gone. We would miss the only time of the year when the landscape becomes a sheet of paper and all upon it the dark lines of pen, only here and there a watercolor touch of faded brown or that particular orange of a winter's setting sun when it lights the final twilight glow along the horizon.

Peter Loewer, *Garden Almanac*

FLOWERS OF THE MIND

AST winter when I was in bed with the 'Flu
And a temperature of a hundred and two,
I was telling the gardener what he should do.

You must keep the *Neurosis* well watered, I said.
Be certain to weed my *Anaemia* bed.
That yellow *Myopsis* is getting too tall,
Tie up the *Lumbago* that grows on the wall.
Those scarlet *Convulsions* are quite a disgrace,
They're like the *Deliriums* — all over the place.
The pink *Pyorrhoea* is covered with blight,
That golden *Arthritis* has died in the night.
Those little dwarf *Asthmas* are nearly in bloom —

But just then the doctor came into the room.

— Reginald Arkell, *Green Fingers*

GARDENERS CHARACTERISTICS

ardeners display a set of characteristics that are rare in the population as a whole. They remain optimistic, even cheerful, in the face of overwhelming odds against their success. They marvel endlessly at simple and fleeting events of a sort that rarely end up in the newspapers — the opening of a peony flower, for example, or the way a dogwood's branches hold the snow in winter. Gardeners are generous with their ideas, even more so with their possessions. Visit a gardener and you will leave with your head full of ideas and your pockets brimming with cuttings and the like.

— Thomas C. Cooper, *Horticulture* magazine

SNOW-ON-THE-MOUNTAIN

hat beautiful names we have given many plants which are poisonous — snow-on-the-mountain, star-of-Bethlehem, larkspur, bleeding heart, wake-robin, honeysuckle. It was surely done in tribute to their beauty alone, and in ignorance, until recent times, of their toxic properties. For other poisonous plants have common names (as well as their Latin botanical names) which act as warning signs: cursed crowfoot, death camass, deadly nightshade, locoweed and so on. The English name of the order to which snow-on-the-mountain belongs — spurge — comes from an Old French word meaning to purge, and that describes one of the effects the plant has on the digestive system . . .

— Hubert Creekmore, *Daffodils are Dangerous*

The Well-equipped Gardener

hen I'm asked how I choose tools, I tell people I buy the very best quality I can afford. I am a New England Yankee, and as a group we have a reputation for being frugal. A Yankee is not apt to spend any money unless he can see he's investing in something of real value. So I buy the best quality equipment I can find, because I know that's by far the cheapest way in the long run. I want tools I can depend on. Thus, I always advise that before you buy any tool, pick it up and examine it carefully. Does the workmanship look sloppy? If so, pass it by immediately. If not, see how the tool is constructed: Are stress points reinforced? What kind of metal is used? Is the tool finished carefully? . . . You know you've made the right choice when suddenly you just can't wait to get out in the garden and start working. Any tool that stimulates such feelings will soon become indispensable.

— James Underwood Crockett, *Crockett's Tool Shed*

Bulbs are Fascinating Perennials

ulbs are a fascinating category of perennial plants. Their lumpy underground structure is designed to get them through hard times, whether winter cold or summer drought. It also makes them relatively easy to ship to market and plant in the garden. And what a diverse category of plants. There are bulbs for shady woodlands and sunny open areas, regions with mild winters and those with cold ones, locations with limited rainfall and others where precipitation is more abundant. Not all bulbs are winter hardy, or able to flower where winters are warm. But that doesn't stop dedicated gardeners, as many bulbs can be stored over harsh winters, refrigerated or stored in containers.

— Judy Glattstein, *Gardener's World of Bulbs*

HONESTY

The Puritans called it "honesty" and took it to Massachusetts and planted it in their first gardens. Why? It was not grown for food, nor was it an herb for healing ills or seasoning food. It added nothing whatever to the welfare of the colony. There seems to be but one excuse for such worldly indulgence — that honesty sustained homesick hearts through the first bitter winters. Bouquets of its silvery pods decorated mantels and corner cupboards — nostalgic symbols of former gaiety. Vanity? Perhaps. But generations have smiled and noted ironically that the only seed the Pilgrims brought to New England was honesty. The sentiment with which it was regarded is conveyed by the folk names that still cling to it. Some sound mercenary: "silver penny," "moneywort," "money-in-the-pocket," "pennyflower," and "moneyseed." Others are more descriptive: "white satin," "satin seed," "satinpod." But honesty acquired an older name — "prick-song flower," which suggests song fests in early English homes — from the needle-sharp point on each seed pod, which was once used to prick out notes of songs on thin paper, a common practice before music was printed . . .

— Claire Shaver Haughton, *Green Immigrants*

ORNAMENTAL GRASSES

G rasses have always graced the natural landscapes of the earth. Now they are coming into our gardens, bringing sound, movement, lush volume and abiding color. Versatile ornamental grasses serve in every garden capacity. They are fillers and specimens, meadow and border subjects, screening material and container plants. They belong to no particular style or era but, ageless, embody the ideal expression of each style and every garden . . . Ornamental grasses growing in stylized meadows seem to be the signature plants of a new age of gardening. Yet when they are placed in another setting with different companion plants, when they are repeated in rhythmic intervals within ribbons of annual color, or when they cascade from antique urns, they become fitting inhabitants of a Victorian pattern garden.

— Carol Ottesen, *Ornamental Grasses*

POTTED PLANTS

lants in pots are like animals in a zoo — they're totally dependent on their keepers.

— John Van de Water, *Star-Ledger*

SOURCE NOTES AND COPYRIGHT NOTICES

Page 11:   From *Being There* by Jerzy Kosinski. © 1970 by Jerzy Kosinski. Courtesy of Harcourt Brace Jovanovich.

Page 13:   From *Autumn Across America* by Edwin Way Teale. © 1956 by Edwin Way Teale. Reprinted by permission of Dodd Mead & Co.

Page 15:   From *Dirt* by Dianne Benson. © 1994 by Dianne C. Benson. Reprinted by permission of Dell Publishing Co.

Page 16:   From *Henry IV* by William Shakespeare. Public domain.

Page 19:   From *The Gardener's Year* by Karel Capek. © 1929 by George Allen & Unwin Ltd. Reprinted by permission.

Page 21:   From *The Complete Book of Edible Landscaping* by Rosalind Creasy. © 1982 by Rosalind Creasy. Reprinted by permission of The Sierra Club.

Page 23:   From *Trinity* by Leon Uris. © 1976 by Leon Uris. Courtesy of Doubleday/Bantam Books.

Page 25:   From *Reuben, Reuben* by Peter deVries. Published by arrangement and reprinted by permission of Little, Brown and Company.

Page 27:   Excerpt from *Self*, "How My Garden and I Grow," by Lisa Germany. *Self*, May 1996, p. 184. Reprinted by permission.

Page 29:   From *The Countryman's Year* by David Grayson. © 1936 by Doubleday, Doran. Copyright © 1985 by James Stannard Baker, Roger Denlo Baker, Judith MacDonald, Beal Baker Hyde, Renaissance House Publishers — a division of Jende-Hagan Inc.

Page 31:   From *Gardening on Main Street* by Buckner Hollingsworth. © 1968 by Rutgers University Press. Courtesy of Rutgers University Press.

Page 33:   Excerpt from *Garden Design*, "Gardeners," by Dorothy Kalins. *Garden Design*, Dec./Jan. 1996, p. 6. Reprinted by permission.

Page 35:   From the *New Testament*, Matthew, vi, 28, 29; Luke, xii, 27.

Page 37:   Excerpt from "April," *Martha Stewart Living*, April 1996, p. 87. Reprinted by permission.

Page 39:   From *The Education of a Gardener* by Russell Page. © 1962 by Russell Page. Courtesy of Random House.

Page 41:   From *Acres and Pains* by S. J. Perelman. © 1943 by S. J. Perelman. Reprinted by permission of Reynal & Hitchcock.

Page 43:   From *The Seasons of America Past* by Eric Sloane. © 1958 by Wilfred Funk. Reprinted by permission.

Page 45:   From *The World is Round* by Gertrude Stein. © 1939 by Gertrude Stein. Renewed © 1967 by the Estate of Gertrude Stein. Courtesy of North Point Press.

Page 47:   From *Onward and Upward in the Garden* by Katherine S. White. © 1958-79 by E. B. White, executor of the estate of Katherine S. White. Reprinted by permission of Farrar, Straus, Giroux.

Page 49:   From *Popular Flowering Plants* by H. L. V. Fletcher. © 1971 by H. L. V. Fletcher. Courtesy of Drake Publishers.

Page 51:   From *I Wandered Lonely as a Cloud: Poems of the Imagination*, no. xii, by William Wordsworth.

Page 53:   From *My Summer in a Garden* by Charles Dudley Warner. © 1885 by Houghton Mifflin. Courtesy of Houghton Mifflin.

Page 55:   From *This Hill, This Valley* by Hal Borland. © 1957 by Hal Borland. Reprinted by permission of Simon & Schuster.

Page 56:   From *Harrowsmith*, "Summer Squash," by Roger B. Swain. *Harrowsmith*, Jan./Feb. 1986, p. 75. © 1985 by Camden House.

Page 59:   From *Green Fingers* by Reginald Arkell. © 1936 by Dodd, Mead & Co. Reprinted by permission.

Page 61:   From *A Joy of Gardening* by Hilaire Belloc. © 1958 by Harper and Brothers. Courtesy of Harper and Brothers.

Page 63:   From *Betty Crocker's Kitchen Garden* by Mary Mason Campbell. © 1971 by Western Publishing Co., published under license from General Mills. Courtesy of Western Publishing Co.

Page 65:   From *Places*, Colette. © 1971 Bobbs-Merrill Co., English translation, © Peter Owen, Bobbs-Merrill Co. Reprinted by permission.

Page 67: From *First Garden* by Truman Capote. © 1976 by Lucy Cochrane Guest, G. P. Putnam's Sons. Copyright © 1976 by Lucy Cochrane Guest. Reprinted by permission of Chanticleer Press.

Page 69: From *Theme Gardens* by Barbara Damrosch. © 1982 by Barbara Damrosch. Reprinted by permission of Workman Publishing Co.

Page 71: From *Garden Wizardry* by Richard C. Davids. © 1976 by Richard C. Davids. Courtesy of Crown Publishers.

Page 73: From *The Natural Garden* by Ken Druse. © 1989 by Ken Druse. Reprinted by permission of Clarkson Potter.

Page 75: From *The Years in My Herb Garden* by Helen M. Fox. © 1953 by The Macmillan Co. Courtesy of Macmillan Co.

Page 77: From *Landscaping with Vines* by Frances Howard. © 1959 by Frances Howard. Courtesy of Macmillan Co.

Page 79: From *A Joy of Gardening* by Vita Sackville-West. © 1958 by Harper and Brothers. Courtesy of Harper and Brothers.

Page 81: From *Masters of the Victory Garden* by Jim Wilson. © 1990 by Little, Brown and Co., WGBH Educational Foundation, Jim Wilson and Russell Morash. Courtesy of Little, Brown and Co.

Page 83: From *The Complete Book of Pitfalls* by Dereck Williamson. © 1971 by McCall Publishing Co.

Page 85: From *Delights and Prejudices* by James Beard. © 1964 by James Beard.

Page 86: From *To Autumn*, Book of Quotations by William Blake.

Page 89: From *Gardens are for People* by Thomas D. Church.

Page 91: From *Stalking the Wild Asparagus* by Euell Gibbons. © 1962 by Euell Gibbons. Courtesy of David McKay Co. Inc.

Page 93: From *Colour Schemes for the Flower Garden* by Gertrude Jekyll. Pub. 1908, London Country Life, Ltd. and pub. 1983, The Ayer Company. Courtesy of The Ayer Company.

Page 95: From *After the Spring*, "The Attractions of Gardening," by Arthur Miller. *After the Spring House & Garden,* April 1983, p. 105. Reprinted by permission.

Page 97: From *Faith in a Seed* by Henry David Thoreau. © 1993 by Island Press, Washington, DC.

Page 99: From *Onward and Upward in the Garden* by Katherine S. White. © 1958-79 by E. B. White, executor of the estate of Katherine S. White. Courtesy of Farrar, Straus, Giroux.

Page 101: From *Making Things Grow* by Thalassa Cruso. © 1960 by Thalassa Cruso. Courtesy of AA Knopf.

Page 103: From *Versus* by Ogden Nash. © 1939-49 by Ogden Nash. Reprinted by permission of Little Brown & Co.

Page 105: From *Greenprints*, "With My Own Hands," by Ralph Waldo Emerson. *Greenprints,* Spring 1990, p. 31.

Page 107: From *The Adventurous* by Christopher Lloyd. © 1983 by Christopher Lloyd. Published in UK by Allen Lane, © 1983 Penguin Books. Courtesy of Vintage Press/Random House.

Page 108: From *Garden Almanac* by Peter Loewer. © 1983 by Peter Loewer. Reprinted by permission of Putnam Publishing Group.

Page 111: Excerpt from *Green Fingers*, "Flowers on the Mind," by Reginald Arkell. © 1936 by Dodd, Mead & Co. Reprinted by permission.

Page 113: *Horticulture*, "Gardeners Characteristics," by Thomas C. Cooper. *Horticulture,* Dec. 1986, p. 4.

Page 115: From *Daffodils are Dangerous* by Hubert Creekmore. © 1966 by Hubert Creekmore. Courtesy of Walker & Co.

Page 117: From *Crockett's Tool Shed* by James Underwood Crockett. © 1979 by Birch Meadow Farms, Inc. Courtesy of Little, Brown & Co.

Page 119: From *Gardener's World of Bulbs*, forward by Judy Glattstein. © 1991 by Brooklyn Botanic Garden. Reprinted by permission.

Page 121: From *Green Immigrants* by Claire Shaver Haughton. © 1978 by Claire Shaver Haughton. Reprinted by permission of Harvest/Harcourt Brace Jovanovich.

Page 123: From *Ornamental Grasses* by Carol Ottesen. © 1989 by Carol Ottesen. Courtesy of McGraw Hill.

Page 125: Excerpt from *Star-Ledger*, "Potted Plants," by John Van de Water. "Beauty Parlor," *Star-Ledger,* Aug. 25, 1996, p. 12.